MORE LAST DAYS OF STEAM AROUND
LONDON

Ten of the 'Standard' 9F 2–10–0 freight locomotives were built with the Italian style of Crosti boiler for comparative purposes, all being allocated to Wellingborough (15A) when new. In later years the lower pre-heater boiler was blanked off and the chimney removed from the offside, but the series still offered a unique appearance to British eyes. No. 92021 of Kettering (15B) stood alongside 4–6–2 No. 70017 *Arrow* one December morning in 1963.

Author

MORE LAST DAYS OF STEAM AROUND
LONDON

D. FEREDAY GLENN

ALAN SUTTON

First published in the United Kingdom in 1992 by
Alan Sutton Publishing Ltd · Phoenix Mill · Stroud · Gloucestershire

First published in the United States of America in 1992 by
Alan Sutton Publishing Inc · Wolfeboro Falls · NH 03896–0848

British Library Cataloguing in Publication Data

Glenn, David Fereday
More Last Days of Steam Around London
I. Title
625.26109421

ISBN 0–86299–916–2

Library of Congress Cataloging in Publication Data applied for

Jacket photographs: Top: For their farewell tour, a brace of Beattie 2–4–0WT locomotives built in 1874 ran from Waterloo to Hampton Court on 2.12.62; Nos. 30585 and 30587 shuffled into Surbiton with steam to spare, having outlived all but one of their class by more than sixty years; Centre: Resplendent in lined Brunswick Green 'Large Prairie' 2–6–2T No. 6117 was taking water at Aylesbury after arrival with a train from High Wycombe on 13.3.62. The shed can be seen in the background; Bottom: Numbered 33 in the Departmental stock of Eastern Region, this class Y4 0–4–0T was the last survivor of five built for the Great Eastern Railway. Previously No. 68129, the short-wheelbase shunter was active at Stratford on 21.6.62.

Endpapers: Front: Though at first sight the O1 class 0–6–0 might be mistaken for a Wainwright C, closer inspection revealed it to be a much older design that originated on the South Eastern Railway in 1878. No. 31048 had a good head of steam on 15.2.58 as it made ready to leave Stewarts Lane; of the handful of survivors at that period it was the only example to have the smaller (5 ft 1 in diameter) driving wheels; Back: Classic 'turn of the century' steam locomotive, class C 0–6–0 No. 31317, at home at Stewarts Lane (73A) against the backdrop of the Decca building on 19.3.61.

Typeset in 9/10 Palatino.
Typesetting and origination by
Alan Sutton Publishing Limited.
Printed in Great Britain by
The Bath Press, Avon.

Introduction

Dr Johnson wrote:

> When a man is tired of London, he is tired of life; for there is in London all that life can afford.

While he penned these words in 1777 – a little before the age of railways – such an observation would still have been entirely apt in the first two decades after National-ization. As a prelude to this second volume about London in the well-established Last Days of Steam series, may I pay tribute to the pioneering work by Kevin Robertson in the original (published in 1988). It is a measure of the abundance of material that exists about the railways in and around the Metropolis that I have been able to garner a further selection, this time largely from my own sources, without being (I trust) repetitious.

Before the Grouping of the railways into the 'Big Four' in 1923 there had been an extensive number of systems seeking access to London, and something of their individuality managed to linger right through into the British Railways period. Severely run-down and underfunded after the depredations of the Second World War, many stations and most locomotive depots in the London area presented a dismal appearance that changed little until the abandonment of steam power. The sad fact is that, with the elimination of the 'puffers', much of the character and charm of old London went too. One has only to think of the Doric Arch that once graced Euston, of Nine Elms depot (where the New Covent Garden Market now stands) or Feltham Hump shunting yard near Heathrow Airport. . . . The capital may no longer suffer from infamous 'smog' (that lethal combination of sulphureous fumes and fog) but the place is not noticeably cleaner overall. A different kind of pollution pervades the atmosphere now that motor bus and car – particularly the private car – have ousted the tram and trolley bus from the streets. A passenger arriving at Paddington station in the last days of Brunel's Broad Gauge might still recognize the place one hundred years later, for the overhead catenary has not yet penetrated that august terminus; St Pancras, too, might be identifiable but the rest have changed out of all conscience.

I can dimly remember trams in London from a childhood treat in the late 1940s. Then, much more clearly, there are memories of rare visits with fellow pupils from the Railway Club at Churcher's College in the fifties, when a Southdown coach from Petersfield took us to see the wonders of King's Cross (Top Shed), Stratford, Bricklayers Arms and Stewarts Lane depots. Another time we included Nine Elms, Norwood Junction and Hither Green in an orgy of loco-spotting, the back streets of south London causing the coach driver some anxious moments when trying to locate obscure entrances to attractions with which he was not familiar. But it was during these shed visits that my interest in the railway moved on from mere number-taking to portraiture, trying to record on film just a few of the myriads of steam engines encountered at that time. The first camera I used was reliable only with 'still' subjects – even then, a perfectly good picture could sometimes be spoiled by an intermittent fault in the bellows. By 1955 I had a Purma, which gave sixteen half-frame negatives on 127 film, but it was hopeless for scenes inside the shed. Not until Christmas 1956 was the matter resolved to my satisfaction, when I was given a Zeiss Ikon Nettar producing twelve 2¼ inch square negatives on 120 film: it was with this camera that most of my monochrome pictures were taken, and it is in occasional use even today. If only it had been available a few years earlier. . . .

As usual, thanks are due to Margaret Lovell for her unfailing help in providing a 'second opinion' in the selection of pictures, plus a critical eye over the wording of the captions. Having commuted to London daily as a student thirty years ago, to have started to do so again in the 1980s brought a fresh perspective to one's knowledge: old landmarks in some places were still discernable, while in others it was as though they had never existed at all. The establishment of Network South-East – putting all the

A glimpse of the Industrial Revolution before the railways: opened in 1820 by the Regent's Canal Company, this new cut linked the busy Paddington Arm of the Grand Junction Canal with Limehouse Basin and the River Thames, becoming part of the Grand Union Canal in 1929. St Pancras locks are in the foreground of this picture, with the station of the same name beyond – note the 'Blood and custard' livery of some of the carriages in the background. These locks effectively divide St Pancras from King's Cross station. The date is 12.4.58.

Author

surviving British Railways' lines in the Greater London area under one operational structure for the first time – has served to hasten the pace of change still further with a new 'corporate image'. Continued expansion of electrification has raised the possibility of overhead gantries even in that most conservative of terminals, Paddington – but only for suburban services, so far! Waterloo is still reeling from the impact of the Channel Tunnel developments, while King's Cross also has that prospect of international traffic looming for the future. Underground, overground, Crossrail . . . London has another exciting decade ahead.

Finally, a word about the Last Days of Steam. This series of volumes never envisaged limiting coverage *exclusively* to steam-powered trains, and in the case of London it is worth making the point that the world's first electric tube railway was opened there in 1890 (City and South London). Also, perhaps surprisingly, London Transport continued to rely on steam for certain engineers' trains over parts of the Underground network until 1971, almost four years *after* the disappearance of such motive power from Waterloo – the last British Rail terminal to feature steam in the capital. The place was continually in a state of flux, and I have tried to illustrate both routine and particular aspects of the changing scene as it occurred from Nationalization in 1948 until steam's 'official' last gasp in 1971. More recent commemorative events, such as Woking 150, and the periodic steam specials from Marylebone have no place in this volume, but we can all take comfort from the fact that steam has somehow bridged the generation gap and continues to give delight to young and old alike – not only in London but in the country at large.

More than fifty years of electric tramway operation came to an end in London on 5.7.52. One of the standard E/1 bogie cars, No. 1927, was running along a conduit section of track near Waterloo during the final week, passing a new London Transport Leyland double-deck bus (RTL 451). Note the bridge advertisement for Wills' Woodbine cigarettes!

Alan B. Cross

The Thames has provided a last mooring place for several survivors from a bygone age of steam propulsion. P.S. *Tattershall Castle* is now berthed alongside Embankment, just upstream from Hungerford Bridge and Charing Cross terminus, having found a new lease of life as a floating restaurant and bar.

Author

Locomotive Depots

One of the benefits to emerge soon after the Nationalization of Britain's four main railway companies on 1 January 1948 was a comprehensive system of shed codes for the multitude of steam Motive Power Depots. Based on the former London Midland and Scottish Railway scheme, every shed from Penzance to Wick was included in the alpha-numeric system. The codes were allocated in accordance with Regional boundaries, with no attempt at rationalization – that would have been much too avant-garde – so, while Willesden Junction was numbered 1A, neighbouring Neasden was 34E simply because it came under a different Region's control. Likewise, Old Oak Common's code was 81A since it belonged to the Western Region, whose block of numbers was the highest in the scheme, in spite of the depot being even nearer to Willesden than Neasden! But all this variety in no way diminished the interest that engine sheds and locomotive allocations aroused among students of British Railways – either at the time or, indeed, many years afterwards.

My own fascination with Motive Power Depots was aroused when peering between the railings that separated Goldsmith Avenue from Fratton shed one day in 1948; curiosity was fanned into enthusiasm while exploring Eastleigh on New Year's Eve 1949. Who could forget the amazing spectacle of what seemed like hundreds of hissing monsters, lit only by a few weak electric bulbs inside the vast smoke-ridden edifice and an occasional glow from ash-pan or firebox? As one shuffled between the rows of engines there were all sorts of hidden traps for the unwary, underfoot: puddles of water, a coil of hosepipe or an unseen heap of firebars, and all coated in a generous layer of soot or grease. Hardly anyone could emerge from such a place unscathed, but it says much for the timeless appeal of steam that people came back again and again. After all, some folk even *worked* there! As a pupil at a boarding school in the provinces, the opportunity to visit London for a day's 'shed-bashing' was a singular delight to be savoured like a glass of wine at Christmas – the most likely occasion for such an outing being at the end of the summer term, around mid-July. To be entertained at all, at least one member of the teaching staff had to be won over to the idea of supervising a party of twenty to thirty boys, but this never proved insurmountable (in my experience). Then a coach had to be hired for the day, to collect the intrepid enthusiasts from school and bring them safely home again, and a picnic lunch would be provided for all concerned. Finally, arrangements had to be made for shed permits well in advance, and this might entail requests being made to two or three of the four Regions that served London – it was found impractical to attempt to visit more than three depots starting from as far afield as Petersfield.

In this volume I have not attempted exhaustive coverage of the sheds within the Greater London area, but rather a taste here and there of some of the sights and locomotive types to be discovered during the final years of steam. A complete list of depots extant in 1951 follows.

LONDON MIDLAND REGION	1A	Willesden Junction
	1B	Camden
	1C	Watford
	1D	Devons Road (Bow)
	14A	Cricklewood
	14B	Kentish Town
	14C	St Albans
EASTERN REGION	30A	Stratford (with sub-sheds at Brentwood, Chelmsford, Epping, Spitalfields, Wood Street, Palace Gates, Enfield Town and Ware)
	30B	Hertford East (with sub-shed at Buntingford)
	30C	Bishops Stortford
	33A	Plaistow (with sub-shed at Upminster)
	33B	Tilbury
	34A	King's Cross
	34B	Hornsey
	34C	Hatfield
	34D	Hitchin
	34E	Neasden (with sub-sheds at Aylesbury and Chesham)
SOUTHERN REGION	70A	Nine Elms
	70B	Feltham
	70C	Guildford (with sub-sheds at Bordon and Ash)
	70D	Basingstoke
	70E	Reading
	73A	Stewarts Lane
	73B	Bricklayers Arms
	73C	Hither Green
	75C	Norwood Junction
WESTERN REGION	81A	Old Oak Common
	81B	Slough (with sub-sheds at Aylesbury, Marlow and Watlington)
	81C	Southall (with sub-shed at Staines)
	81D	Reading (with sub-sheds at Basingstoke and Henley-on-Thames)
LONDON TRANSPORT		Neasden (Metropolitan Line)
		Lillie Bridge (District Line)

Something of the Webb tradition of the old London and North Western lingered while cumbersome 7F 0–8–0 tender engines continued to make an appearance. On 9.9.57 No. 49078 exhibited its classic origins with such features as the pattern of smokebox door, driving wheels and tender. Having coaled up and taken on water, this chunky freight locomotive was ready to move off shed for its next assignment.

Author

At most major depots it was usual to find some elderly carriages downgraded for Departmental service; such was the case at Willesden. In December 1963 two corridor vehicles were stabled on a short siding there, the nearer example being of pre-Grouping origin but equipped with simple three-link coupling for ease of shunting.

Author

Gleaming in the winter sunshine, 'Princess Coronation' 'Pacific' No. 46209 *Princess Beatrice* looks every inch a thoroughbred on shed at 1A on 15.2.58. Its home depot appears to be Crewe North (5A), and one would normally expect such a machine to be serviced at Camden (1B) when visiting London. A Fowler 4P 2–6–4T is over the pit alongside.

Author

The Stanier rebuild of Fowler's original 'Royal Scot' class with taper boiler and double chimney from 1943 onwards created a handsome and powerful locomotive that lasted well into the sixties. Designated 7P by the London Midland Region, No. 46138 *The London Irish Rifleman* was out of steam at Willesden on 9.9.57.

Author

A number of the 'Patriot' (or 'Baby Scot') 4–6–0 locomotives had a rebuild similar to that afforded the 'Royal Scot' class. On 20.6.62 No. 45529 *Stephenson* was to be found over the pit outside its home shed, an imposing sight at close quarters especially when viewed from a low angle. Rebuilt examples were classified 7P like their 'Royal Scot' counterparts.

Author

Not all the 'Patriot' class had names: No. 45544 was one of those not so blessed. On an overcast September day in 1957 the Edge Hill (8A) engine was brewing up nicely in preparation for a return to Liverpool, its classic appearance recalling the LNWR 'Claughton' ancestry.

Author

Against the backcloth of industrial NW10, one of the ubiquitous 3F 'Jinty' 0–6–0T engines makes its own contribution to London's polluted atmosphere on 9.9.57. No. 47355, without front number-plate after the fashion of many ex-LNWR machines, storms past lines of 16 and 21 ton steel-bodied wagons on the southern margin of the depot; more than 400 similar engines were built after the Grouping as a development of Johnson's Midland Railway designs.

Author

Even in the late 1950s there was still plenty of work for steam shunting engines to do, despite the onset of dieselization. No. 47501, equipped with vacuum brake and steam heating pipes, was a refugee from one of the country's first all-diesel conversions as it was transferred to Willesden from Devons Road (1D). The weather seemed positively spring-like on 28.2.59.

Author

An oil tank wagon appeared ominously in the shed complex on 9.9.57, but steam was still very much in control at that time. One of the original 1934-series of Stanier 'Black 5' 4–6–0s (No. 45014), with combined small dome and top feed, posed in front of the water tower.

Author

An early Stanier design was the powerful 2–6–0 with taper boiler and combined top feed and dome. It was rare to visit Willesden depot without finding one of these distinctive locomotives in steam – on 28.2.59 the incumbent was No. 42957.

Author

The first LMS 2–6–0 was based on Hughes' Lancashire and Yorkshire Railway design. 245 of these capable machines were built and were to be found all over the system. The steeply-inclined angle of the cylinders earned them the nickname 'Crabs'. No. 42781 appeared among the many wooden-bodied coal wagons on 9.9.57.

Author

A whole range of tank engines used to handle the ECS trains in and out of Euston, in addition to working some of the suburban traffic. Both Fowler and Stanier versions of the 2–6–2T and 2–6–4T (power classification 3 and 4, respectively) were to be seen: Fowler 2–6–2T No. 40051 was at its home depot on 9.9.57.

Author

The characteristic haze that hung over Willesden like a pall was induced by the sulphureous fumes emitted by the many steam locomotives on shed. On a December morning in 1963 those present included 'Britannia' class 'Pacific' No. 70016 *Ariel*. Its shabby, work-worn state was in contrast to the halcyon years in the fifties when it was one of the stars at Cardiff (Canton) shed, 86C. The grab-holes in the smoke deflectors were a relic of its Western Region period.

Author

When Camden (1B) closed, Willesden provided a haven for all the remaining 'quality' steam locomotives. The sight of a red 'Duchess' 4–6–2 among all the black and grey engines was sheer magic! One misty December morning in 1963 No. 46225 *Duchess of Gloucester* stood out from among the rest like a truly regal machine, the hazy sun highlighting its crimson paintwork.

Author

A chance visit to Willesden on 15.2.58 found both of the original LMS diesel 'twins' in residence in the roundhouse. 10000 and 10001 sometimes worked in multiple, and had corridor connections at either end to allow for access to both when coupled together. They had a spell on loan to the Southern in the early 1950s for comparison with Bulleid's trio of main line diesels (10201–3), but eventually all five ran on the London Midland Region out of Euston.

Author

Camden was the shed for the London Midland Region's 'prima donnas', as well as visiting engines from a wide variety of destinations. On 10.11.56 a glittering 'Jubilee' 4–6–0, No. 45653 *Barham* showed the lined Brunswick Green livery to perfection, probably in connection with the annual Remembrance Day service and parades. The same name was carried by a BR-built Peppercorn 'Pacific' (No. 60531, based in Scotland) – one wonders whether they ever met, in Carlisle or Glasgow, perhaps?

Author

A grey November day was brightened by the sight of 'Princess Coronation' 4–6–2, No. 46210 hissing merrily as it left Camden to back down to Euston for a mid-day departure for the North. *Lady Patricia* was decorated with poppies and greenery on the smokebox door on 10.11.56, a heartfelt gesture from railwaymen for their fallen comrades.

Author

First of the London sheds to eliminate steam completely under the Modernization Plan, 1D was given an allocation of Type 1 diesel-electrics of 800 bhp built by B.T.H. The plain, functional lines of D8201 at its home shed on 28.2.59 are a far cry from the old North London 0–6–0Ts that lingered there in the early 1950s; the Brunswick Green paint is relieved only by the bright metalwork and steam-age white headcode discs.

Author

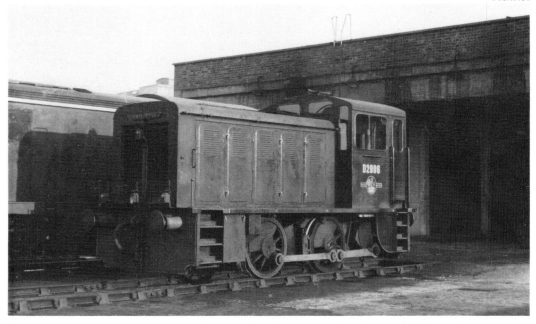

This steam-era depot had a new breed of motive-power by the late 1950s, a four-coupled power-house on wheels developing 330 bhp from a super-charged MAN type diesel engine. D2906 was one of a series from the North British Locomotive Company with hydraulic transmission.

Author

As long ago as 1899, Johnson brought out a large and powerful 0–6–0T for the Midland Railway. After 1919 these engines were modified with the Belpaire firebox, but were otherwise little altered from the day they were built. No. 47211 was one equipped with condensing apparatus specially for the London area, but the entire class (and the post-Grouping 'Jinties') were classified 3F. The distinctive bunker of the later design can be seen on No. 47434 behind.

Author

While the Tilbury line had been part of the LMS after the Grouping, this 4–4–2T locomotive appeared at Stratford for scrapping. No. 41970 was built as a post-Grouping development of the earlier Whitelegg LT&S '79' class for passenger services from Fenchurch Street; it was recorded at 30A on 26.7.55.

Author

The Great Eastern had several classes of 2–4–2T at its disposal, but with the onset of Modernization on BR their days were numbered. One of the push-pull fitted class F5s, No. 67218, was on shed on 1.3.58 shortly before withdrawal.

Author

Known as the 'Big One', Stratford was a vast complex of Motive Power Depot, Works and dump (for engines awaiting scrap). A quaint GER class for which, sadly, there was no reprieve was the J70 six-coupled Tram locomotive. With cow-catchers and enclosed valve gear – when in full working order – Holden's 1903 design was most at home on the Wisbech and Upwell tramway. One of the last to go was No. 68223, at Stratford on 26.7.55.

Author

Since the 1920s the suburban services out of Liverpool Street had been mainly the preserve of a large class of 0–6–2T, first designed by Hill for the GER. Electrification gradually brought about their demise on the 'Jazz' service, as it was known for decades, but class N7 No. 69632 was in steam on 21.6.62 in the company of B1 4–6–0 No. 61149 and a 'Buckjumper' 0–6–0T.

Author

On the Great Northern section out of King's Cross the class N2 0–6–2T held sway. On 1.3.58 No. 69592 was freshly ex-Works at Stratford, being one of the later (N2/4) variety with condensing apparatus. Such engines were used through the tunnels to and from Moorgate – the brackets for a front destination board can be seen projecting from the lower half of the smokebox door.

Author

Holden's 'maid of all work' on the GER might well have been the simple 0–6–0 tender engine that became class J17 in LNER days. Some, like No. 65507, had disproportionately small tenders but that may have had something to do with it not being equipped with vacuum brake (and thus unable to work passenger trains). The date was 14.11.59.

Author

The class J19 0–6–0 had a truly massive appearance, as can be judged from this nearside view of No. 64662 on 1.3.58. Not one of the thirty-five examples survived into preservation, though withdrawals did not begin until 1959. Driving wheels were the 'standard size' for the Great Eastern, with a diameter of 4 ft 11 in.

Author

Doyen of the B17 4–6–0s, No. 61600 *Sandringham* was at Stratford on 1.3.58 well coated in grime. In 1947 the engine had been modified with a class B1 boiler (100A type) but retained the small GE-style tender. Note the Westinghouse pump by the smokebox.

Author

Class B1 4–6–0s were to be found all over the erstwhile LNER, and even visited as far afield as Swindon and the South Coast on occasion. No. 61111 was an indigenous 30A locomotive, so it was not surprising to find it at its home shed on 1.3.58. It was a true mixed-traffic machine, equally at ease with passenger or freight haulage.

Author

At the lower end of Stratford's assortment of motive power could be found various classes of 'Buckjumper' 0–6–0T. Of the J66, J67, J68 and J69 variants, the last was the most prolific. On 21.6.62 class J69 No. 68556 was in steam beside the huge coaling stage, this example featuring enlarged side tanks.

Author

Stratford's coaling stage was always a good location for finding engines in steam. In a trio of tanks that included an N7 0–6–2T, an L1 2–6–4T and a 'Buck-jumper', the last was the most unusual since it retained the original flat roof to its cab. By 21.6.62 class J69 No. 68499 was possibly unique in this respect, since it had been on loan in Scotland at a material stage in its existence, so escaping the conversion programme.

Author

The J68 class had the luxury of a side-window cab, but was otherwise almost indistinguishable from the J67/J69 series – Stratford had seen them all. On 14.11.59 J68 No. 68655 simmered in a siding, some wag having put on lamps for the class A headcode!

Author

Stratford Works had an allocation of four Departmental locomotives to deal with internal movements. Three comprised the entire surviving examples of Holden's 1886 design of 0–6–0T for the GER – these became class J66 in the post-Grouping period under LNER auspices. Their BR numbers were 68370, 68378 and 68382, becoming 32, 36 and 31 respectively when transferred to Departmental stock. The first of the trio was tracked down on 21.6.62 shunting a BR Mark 1 carriage still painted in the attractive 'Blood and Custard' livery.

Author

The fourth member of Stratford's stock of Departmental steam shunters was another 'last survivor' in the shape of class Y4 0–4–0T No. 33. Introduced in 1913 by Hill for the GER's requirement for a powerful, short-wheelbase dock tank, it was numbered 68129 on the formation of British Railways, later transferring to the Departmental fleet. It was active outside the Works on 21.6.62, still bearing the chalked nickname of 'Elvis' on the large side tank. By this date it was also BR's last steam 0–4–0T in the London area.

Author

A nearside view of the last class Y4 0–4–0T: fitted with Walschaerts valve gear, Departmental No. 33 had 3 ft 10 in diameter driving wheels and weighed more than 38 tons. Notice how a meagre supply of coal was carried on top of the tank, the cab window being protected by a grille. A pre-Nationalization 350 bhp diesel shunter (12104) was at work in the background.

Author

Just as there had been 'Baby Scot' steam locos, so there were 'Baby Deltic' diesels! On 14.11.59 D5908 was at Stratford, one of only ten Type 2 Bo–Bo machines with electric transmission produced by English Electric for BR that year. Steam era headcode discs were fitted and a corridor-connection facility was built into each 'nose' if the engines were used in multiple.

Author

A funny little 0–4–0 diesel-mechanical shunter caught the eye on 21.6.62. Built by Andrew Barclay, the Gardner engine developed 153 bhp at 1,200 rpm, and a four-speed epicyclic gearbox was fitted. Introduced in 1956, D2956 was originally numbered 11506; the Eastern Region classification was D1/2.

Author

A plentiful supply of 2–6–4T locomotives was required to maintain Tilbury line passenger services before electrification. Brighton-built 4MT No. 80135 was typical of the BR 'Standard' design based at 33A on 28.2.59. Fortunately, this engine has been restored to traffic and now operates on the North Yorkshire Moors line between Grosmont and Pickering.

Author

Last of the former London Tilbury and Southend engines to remain in traffic was 3F 0–6–2T No. 41981, seen inside Plaistow shed on 2.5.59. Fourteen of Whitelegg's '69' class were built from 1903 onwards, primarily for freight haulage, but they were withdrawn rapidly with the onset of dieselization in 1957/8. No. 41981 was fitted with de-icing equipment and reprieved for a time on that account.

Author

The majestic spectacle of a pair of Peppercorn 'Pacifics' preparing for action at Top Shed on 12.4.58: class A1 4–6–2 No. 60156 *Great Central* was one of five such engines to be fitted with roller bearings, while 60145 *Saint Mungo* (from 52A – Gateshead) did not have that refinement.

Author

Several different variants made up the class of A2 'Pacifics'. At Top Shed on 12.4.58 A2/3 No. 60516 *Hycilla* was in sparkling condition in anticipation of some main line duty. The stark double chimney is worthy of note, also the position of the outside cylinders behind the front bogie.

Author

Once a livery policy had been established by British Railways, the class V2 2–6–2 mixed-traffic locomotives were painted in lined black for several years. By 1957 the rigid code was eased somewhat, and No. 60800 *Green Arrow* appeared in the lined Brunswick Green appropriate for such a successful design. On 12.4.58 it stood alongside one of the 9F 2–10–0s at King's Cross shed; today it sees periodic use on special trains restored to LNER Apple Green as 4771.

Author

The oldest type on shed on 12.4.58 was the former Great Northern 0–6–0ST that became class J52. An Ivatt design introduced in 1897, No. 68831 was typical of several that worked in the London area – the chimney and cab were distinctive features. N2 0–6–2Ts were two a penny in those days. . . .

Author

More than a hundred of the standard GNR 0–6–0 designed by Gresley in 1911 were taken over by British Railways. On 25.4.59 at least two were in steam on shed at Hitchin, the example nearest the camera being No. 64251 of class J6. Driving wheels were 5 ft 2 in diameter and a superheated boiler was fitted.

Author

Hitchin (34D) being firmly in Great Northern territory, it was perhaps surprising to find a former GER 0–6–0 based there. On a wet and windy April afternoon in 1959 class J15 0–6–0 No. 65479 had the wisp of smoke from its tall chimney whisked away by the strong sou'wester. This was a Worsdell design of 1883 (modified by Holden) that lasted well into the 1960s.

Author

By 1959 evidence of the Modernization Plan was beginning to appear at Hitchin. Not only was a four-wheel Railbus in use on the branch to Bedford but a diesel shunter had arrived in the shed yard. On 25.4.59 BR-built D2018 was sandwiched between other engines there – its original number was 11205.

Author

As the sun managed to break through the misty, smokey atmosphere of Neasden on 28.2.59 it illuminated the scene outside the shed: locos with coal piled high on tenders or in bunkers, the breakdown crane handy in case of need. In the foreground stood a sad row of engines past their prime, including one designed for the Manchester Sheffield and Lincolnshire Railway from 1891. No. 69257 was an 0–6–2T that was absorbed first by the Great Central, then the LNER and finally BR in a career spanning more than sixty years. It was the only remaining example of class N5 to have been fitted for push-pull working, probably for use on the Chesham branch.

Author

A number of modern 2MT 2–6–2Ts were equipped with push-pull gear to cover the requirements of the Chesham branch, until it was electrified. One of the BR-built engines was No. 41284, simmering in the hazy sunshine outside the shed at 34E on 28.2.59.

Author

A College Railway Club visit to Nine Elms in July 1951 found new 'Britannia Pacific' No. 70009 *Alfred the Great* coaling-up in readiness for working the 'Bournemouth Belle' all-Pullman train from Waterloo at 12.30 p.m. The allocation of a 'Standard' class 7MT 4–6–2 to 70A did not last long, and all too soon the Western Section lost its sole example, though 70004/14 remained at work on the Eastern Section for several more years.

Author

Nine Elms was a historic location from the earliest days of the LSWR, being terminal, Works and loco shed in turn from 1838 to 1967. It was in full view of the main line from Waterloo, and also from residential properties in the south Lambeth area. Though the depot suffered bomb damage during the Second World War, it remained operational until the end of steam on the Southern in July 1967. This view gives some idea of the overall size of Nine Elms in about 1960 – engines on shed include E4, M7 and both rebuilt and original Bulleid 'Pacifics'.

Lens of Sutton

The gargantuan bulk of a class G16 4–8–0T was one of the sights a visitor to 70B might hope to see. Introduced by Urie in 1921 for 'hump' shunting, the 'gang of four' spent a useful existence of more than thirty years performing the work for which they were intended. As diesel shunters began to make inroads into their traditional duties, two were loaned to the Longmoor Military Railway in the 1950s; when they returned, there was even less work for them and half the class was withdrawn. On 5.11.60 No. 30495 still made an impressive picture at its home shed.

Author

At first glance everything in this picture is of pre-Grouping origin. Feltham always had a large allocation of Drummond class 700 'Black Motor' 0–6–0s, and three can be spotted in the background close to the shed building. In the foreground is something even older – an Adams class G6 0–6–0T No. 30349 – but all these ex-LSWR locomotives date from the 1890s. The photograph was taken on Guy Fawkes Day, 1960.

Author

Feltham yard was the starting point for a number of cross-London freight services, so it was not unusual for engines from other parts of the capital to appear there. One of Wainwright's C class 0–6–0 tender engines built for the SECR from 1900, No. 31579, was on shed on 5.11.60 – a type more at home in Surrey or Kent than on the South Western Division.

Author

Bulleids on parade. Just nosing out of the shed on 5.11.60 was one of the ugly 'Utility' class Q1 0–6–0s built to help the war effort, No. 33012, while nearer to the camera a 'Battle of Britain' 4–6–2 had the safety valves lifting exuberantly. No. 34054 *Lord Beaverbrook* was never rebuilt, and was displaying the headcode for Southampton Docks via Chertsey as it prepared to move off shed.

Author

Totally at home at Feltham were Urie's hefty 'Pacific' tanks of class H16. Though the five examples built in 1921 spent almost their entire lives based in the London area, a successful test with No. 30516 on the Fawley branch in March 1960 meant some dispersal to pastures new. Nevertheless, on 5.11.60 No. 30520 was still at 70B; the class was withdrawn *en bloc* at the end of 1962.

Author

Can't you just hear it? Class G16 4–8–0T No. 30494 blasts out of Feltham yard with a cross-London freight on 5.11.60, most likely bound for Willesden via Kew East junction. At this date two of the four giants remained in traffic.

Author

More than 96 tons of tank engine on the move at close quarters! Class H16 4–6–2T No. 30518 accelerates past Guildford's roundhouse turntable on its way to pick up another freight on 23.11.57, its 70B shedplate clearly visible on the smokebox door.

Author

Some of the 'Standard' class 5MT 4–6–0s allocated to the Southern Region were invested with names formerly carried by withdrawn 'King Arthur' N15s. No. 73110 carried the name *The Red Knight* during the early 1960s (previously borne by Urie 4–6–0 No. 30755), but by 2.2.66 the nameplate had been removed.

Author

With three decades of dominance on cross-London freight traffic drawing to a close, class W 2–6–4T No. 31918 stood in front of the vast Decca building as it waited to leave the shed yard on another duty on 19.3.61. These handsome three-cylinder tanks were constructed from kits of parts produced by Woolwich Arsenal, being very similar to the N1 2–6–0 tender engine but specifically limited to freight haulage.

Author

Only eight P class 0–6–0Ts were constructed for the SECR, but their intended purpose on push-pull passenger trains did not last long and they gravitated to shunting. As many as four have been preserved, but No. 31558 (seen in the shed yard on 26.7.55) was not one of the lucky ones.

Author

The 'Lane' had a justified reputation for the cleanliness of its main line locomotives (especially those used on the 'Golden Arrow') but sometimes lesser engines also got first-class treatment. Class H 0–4–4T No. 31261, a 'Chatham' product from the Edwardian years, looked very smart on 26.7.55 as it prepared to leave the yard at 73A.

Author

Though at first sight the O1 class 0–6–0 might be mistaken for a Wainwright C, closer inspection revealed it to be a much older design that originated on the South Eastern Railway in 1878. No. 31048 had a good head of steam on 15.2.58 as it made ready to leave Stewarts Lane; of the handful of survivors at that period it was the only example to have the smaller (5 ft 1 in diameter) driving wheels.

Author

One of the sixty-six Wainwright H class 0–4–4T locomotives that served the SECR and its successors so well until the sixties. No. 31550 was not one of the batch modified for push-pull working after Nationalization; the still-unrebuilt 'Merchant Navy' 4–6–2 *Clan Line* (35028) can be seen in the background on 15.2.58.

Author

Close-up of a very tidy Wainwright C class 0–6–0 in July 1952 (No. 31297). Weighing only 44 tons and with driving wheels of 5 ft 2 in diameter, it was not surprising that such a simple, go-anywhere locomotive design lingered until the twilight of steam. No. 31592, built at Longhedge Works in 1901, is now preserved on the Bluebell Railway in Sussex.

Author

Prototype of the three-cylinder version of Maunsell's mixed-traffic 'Mogul' with 5 ft 6 in driving wheels, No. 31822 was built for the SECR in 1922. On 26.7.55 this engine was at 73C being prepared for the evening rush-hour on duty 176.

Author

It was a surprise to find W class 2–6–4T No. 31916 still showing signs of its pre-Nationalization ownership at Hither Green on 26.7.55. The 'SOUTHERN' was in faded Bulleid-style 'Sunshine' lettering with bunker-side numbers to match, although the figure '3' had been added to comply with BR renumbering.

Author

The following notes of the various locomotives seen at Hither Green, either on shed or hauling trains passing the depot, during the visit of Churcher's College Railway Club on 26 July 1955 may be of interest to readers. They are listed in the order in which they were noted down, as our party of pupils and master-in-charge explored each shed road in turn. For ease of reference, the class of each steam loco is added in brackets after the number and wheelbase notation. Some thirty-seven years afterwards, one can only marvel at the quantity and sheer diversity to be observed at that period in the space of no more than one hour during a weekday afternoon.

31913	2–6–4T	(W)	31816	2–6–0	(N)	
31877	2–6–0	(NI)	31916	2–6–4T	(W)	
31061	0–6–0	(C)	(see opposite, below)			
31059	0–6–0	(C)	34078	4–6–2	(BB)	*222 Squadron*
31861	2–6–0	(N)	DS1173	0–6–0D		
31694	0–6–0	(C)	(Drewery 204 bhp diesel mechanical shunter)			
31924	2–6–4T	(W)	31498	0–6–0	(C)	
31690	0–6–0	(C)	31822	2–6–0	(NI)	
31858	2–6–0	(N)	(see opposite, above)			
31583	0–6–0	(C)	30908	4–4–0	(V)	*Westminster*
31480	0–6–0	(C)	31860	2–6–0	(N)	
15225	0–6–0D		31584	0–6–0	(C)	
(Bulleid/English Electric diesel shunter)			31054	0–6–0	(C)	
31911	2–6–4T	(W)	31294	0–6–0	(C)	
15223	0–6–0D		33037	0–6–0	(QI)	
(Bulleid/English Electric diesel shunter)			31487	4–4–0	(DI)	
31063	0–6–0	(C)	31925	2–6–4T	(W)	
31923	2–6–4T	(W)	30903	4–4–0	(V)	*Charterhouse*

On 15.2.58 the shed building at 75C was almost deserted, but some of the regular occupants were to be seen outside. Class E6 0–6–2T No. 32416 represented the Billinton LBSCR design of 1904, having 4 ft 6 in driving wheels for freight work. This particular locomotive had been allocated to Eastleigh depot (71A) until the early 1950s for use on the Fawley branch oil trains.

Author

With electrification being extended on the Southern Railway to include main lines (such as to Brighton and Portsmouth) as well as suburban routes, three 350 bhp diesel-electric shunting engines were added to stock in the late 1930s. Originally numbered 1, by 15.2.58 15201 looked rather quaint compared with the standard BR shunters, but it survived until 1964 (latterly at Eastleigh).

Author

With orders commencing in 1917 for the SECR, by the 1930s the Southern had accumulated eighty of the two-cylinder class N 'Moguls' for mixed-traffic work all over the system. No. 31871 was at Norwood Junction on 15.2.58

Author

Old loyalties die hard! Belief in God's Wonderful Railway was such that, some fourteen years after Nationalization, it was possible to discern the initials 'GWR' on the flanks of condensing pannier tank 9709. There were eleven of these special versions of the standard 57xx 0–6–0PT, all based at 81A for use through the tunnels of the London Transport Metropolitan Line. With the steam specials that operate on parts of the Underground network from time to time in the 1990s, such an engine would be highly appropriate, but sadly none of this type survived.

Author

On 9.9.57 Old Oak Common yard was bristling with signals but not much else. Standard flat-roofed 0–6–0PT No. 7734 and shunters' truck wait for something to happen. Ring-arm and route indicator signals make an interesting change from the normal pattern Home starter.

Author

Before the days of double chimneys, 4–6–0 No. 6026 *King John* was undergoing routine preparation before being turned to work its next train out of Paddington on 9.9.57. The fire irons leaning against the outside of the cab suggest the footplate and tender were being hosed off, and that departure was not imminent.

Author

Shafts of sunlight filtered through to illuminate parts of the vast double roundhouse that characterized Old Oak. On 9.9.57 the light reflected off the tender of the last active 'Star' class 4–6–0, No. 4056 *Princess Margaret*. The Edwardian era cab showed up clearly.

Author

The analogy between cathedrals and steam depots may be particularly apt in this instance, as the locomotive is No. 5084 *Reading Abbey*. One of several 'Star' class 4–6–0s to be rebuilt by Collett to the 'Castle' specification, No. 5084 gained a further refinement in its last years when it was fitted with a double chimney. The date was 20.6.62.

Author

One of the first of the 'Large Prairie' tank engines to be repainted in Brunswick Green and fully lined out was No. 6135. On 9.9.57 the 2–6–2T was sandwiched between a 'Mogul' and one of the Hawksworth pannier tanks at Old Oak Common – note the copper cap to the chimney on the 61xx series.

Author

The long taper-boiler 2–8–0 was introduced on the Great Western in 1903. No. 2814 was one of the early locomotives of the series and remained at work until the late 1950s; though it had a full tender of coal on 9.9.57 it appeared to be out of steam. While this particular engine went for scrap, several other examples have been preserved, including 2818 for the National Railway Museum at York.

Author

An evocative scene inside a roundhouse at Old Oak Common. Condensing pannier tank No. 9707 was at rest on one of the turntable roads, its chimney beneath one of the vents intended to draw smoke away from the shed and into the open air. The date was 9.9.57.

Author

By 1958 the Modernization Plan was making provision for branch lines with the introduction of single railcars and railbuses, as well as a rolling programme of diesel multiple units of all types for suburban and cross-country traffic. The Western Region's first single cars were manufactured by the Gloucester RC&W Company, with two AEC engines and second-class seating for sixty-five. No. W55011 was in mint condition on 18.10.58, looking a trifle incongruous among the steam-age water towers; this type was later classified as the 122 series.

Author

The Great Western saw the advantages of diesel railcar operation in the thirties and introduced a pilot series of single cars; when these proved successful, a further series capable of hauling a trailer or fitted wagon appeared in 1940, produced in collaboration with AEC at Southall. On 18.10.58 No. W29W of the second batch shared a siding with one of the new Gloucester cars – the GWR car was painted in the attractive Carmine and Cream ('Blood and Custard') livery, while the new railcar was in Brunswick Green with cream lining and 'speed whiskers'. A few ex-Great Western cars ended their days in the green livery in the sixties.

Author

Some London Termini

At the commencement of the twentieth century, by my reckoning there were eleven different main line railway companies (not including those with underground routes that became part of London Transport) operating into the capital. Two of the smaller concerns, the North London and the London, Tilbury and Southend Railway, were absorbed in 1908 and 1912 respectively; the remaining nine continued their separate existence throughout the Great War of 1914–18, but thereafter it was clear that some changes were essential. The 'Grouping' of 1922/3 brought three new major railway companies into being by amalgamation – only the Great Western retained its name from the pioneering days of the 1830s. The remaining eight were consigned to the history books, though not forgotten (especially by their former employees, who maintained the old rivalries long afterwards). So the LSWR, LBSCR and SECR (itself an amalgam of the former South Eastern and London, Chatham and Dover) became the Southern Railway; the Great Central, Great Eastern and Great Northern (with others further north) became the London and North Eastern Railway. Having had some degree of rationalization before 1914, only the Midland and the LNWR (plus others further north) were left to form the London Midland and Scottish Railway.

The 'Big Four', as they became known, did not begin to develop any real identity of their own until after the Depression of the early thirties – and that exciting period was abruptly cut short by Hitler's ambitions across the Channel. Trying to pick up the threads after six years of devastation stretched resources to a point where political dogma won the argument by Nationalization. But British Railways took its time formulating a corporate image (or series of images) while much of the infrastructure remained in the straightjacket of wartime austerity, or worse. Some of London's stations, even important termini, had been allowed to run down to a point where urgent improvements were needed, but the cure of the age was sometimes worse than the disease! Public sympathy for historic buildings and more traditional architecture and materials came too late for some to be saved, so these pictures may recall more than mere items of rolling stock. They are essentially a moment of history: London in the post-war years.

As a 'retired' commuter who has always lived south of the Thames, it would have been natural for me to terminate at Waterloo or Victoria, so I should like to crave readers' indulgence for starting with the Southern, at Waterloo. On the other hand, Waterloo (East) is not included here since it is not a terminal but an intermediate station.

The empty stock duties in and out of Waterloo were for years the responsibility of the ageing Drummond M7 0–4–4Ts. Built in 1897, No. 30248 was going about its usual business when recorded at the 'country' end of platform 9 on 12.4.61; three months later it was withdrawn for scrap. Fortunately, No. 245 (30245) of the 1897 intake and No. 53 (30053) of the later variety adapted for push-pull duties have been preserved out of a class of 105 engines.

Author

Following the success of the 'Radial' excursion in 1961, the Railway Enthusiasts Club was prompted to follow it up with another 'Adams Special' the following year. On 25.3.62 one of the last class O2 0–4–4Ts on the mainland, No. 30199, did a tour of south London suburban lines with a trio of non-corridor coaches borrowed from the London Midland Region – this was the scene before departure from Waterloo. In the fifties No. 30199 had been based at Wadebridge.

Author

Excitement at platform 16: on 19.3.61 a special last excursion to Windsor was operated by the oldest surviving Adams 'Radial' 4–4–2T. Since LSWR days it had been numbered 125, 0125, 3125 and finally 30582 with more than half its long lifespan spent on the Axminster to Lyme Regis branch line, based at Exmouth Junction shed (72A). After its final overhaul at Eastleigh it emerged with the Drummond boiler previously fitted to 30583 (SR No. 3488).

Author

Until 1961 some carriage shunting duties were the prerogative of a select band of ex-LBSCR class E4 0–6–2Ts. On 12.4.61 No. 32487 was performing with gusto as it started a lengthy rake of Bulleid stock out of the terminus, heading for Clapham Junction as the morning rush was ending. The suburban platforms behind the E4 and the architectural landscape beyond them have been transformed since 1990 by developments connected with Waterloo International.

Author

This cameo of the older Southern suburban electric sets in platforms 17 and 18 is history – not just for the 4–SUB units themselves, but also for this part of Waterloo station. On 9.2.61 flat-fronted unit 4337 (on the left) and bow-ended 4324 each included a modern steel-sided Bulleid carriage in the set, but where have all the passengers gone?

Author

Southern partnership: in platform 7 an eight-coach train of 4–COR 'Nelson' units had arrived from Portsmouth Harbour, while in platform 8 a Bournemouth line service was waiting to depart behind the final Bulleid 'Pacific', No. 34110 *66 Squadron*, built in 1949. Steam ended at Waterloo in 1967, but the pre-war 'Nelsons' lingered on into 1972. This picture was taken on 17.3.55.

Author

A brace of Bulleids at the sharp end: unrebuilt 'West Country' 4–6–2 No. 34105 *Swanage* and rebuilt counterpart No. 34040 *Crewkerne* were coupled together on 31.1.61 before trundling down the line to Nine Elms for servicing. In the right background can be seen the Waterloo signal-box that was demolished thirty years later.

Author

Beyond the complicated trackwork, 'Lord Nelson' class 4–6–0 No. 30857 *Lord Howe* lopes away from the platform ends with the 1.30 p.m. to Bournemouth West on 7.2.61. By this time appearances by members of this famous class were largely restricted to boat trains, so it was pleasant to record one on front-line duty with a rake of Bulleid stock.

Author

No. 34005 *Barnstaple* was the first of the lighter 'West Country' Class 'Pacific' loco-motives to be modified with Walschaerts valve gear and air-smoothed casing removed in 1957. On 12.4.61 it was noted drifting into Waterloo with a morning train from the West of England. It was this engine that inspired a fine 4 mm scale model by Hornby-Dublo in the early 1960s.

Author

Blowing-off impatiently, rebuilt 'Merchant Navy' 4–6–2 No. 35022 *Holland–America Line* heads the Southern Counties Touring Society special train to Exeter, Torrington and Ilfracombe on 12.9.65. By this time most service trains beyond Salisbury were worked by WR 'Warship' diesel-hydraulics, so the opportunity to travel behind steam once again over the Southern's famed West of England main line was popular with enthusiasts. The short parcels bay visible on the left of the picture (beyond which was the former carriage road between platforms 11 and 12) has recently been rebuilt in connection with the anticipated Channel Tunnel international traffic, with the loss of some suburban platforms and the rest moved across and renumbered.

Author

Across Hungerford Bridge stood Charing Cross where, in 1957, could be found examples of steam, diesel and electric trains. While the Hastings line services had mostly been usurped by curious flat-sided six-car DMUs, the elegant 'Schools' 4–4–0s were still in evidence there. On 5.7.57 class V No. 30929 *Malvern* waited to leave with the 11.48. a.m. semi-fast to Ashford, with Maunsell set 214 behind the tender. The engine was painted in lined Brunswick Green.

Author

The original 'short' six-car diesel-electric multiple units for the Charing Cross – Tonbridge – Hastings service inaugurated DMU operation on the Southern in 1957. A handful remained at work early in 1984, including No. 1006 forming a lunchtime service for the East Sussex resort. The slab-sided design to suit the narrow tunnels prevalent between Tunbridge Wells and Hastings is clearly shown; this type was latterly class 201.

Author

The unique double-deck electric train comprised two 4–DD suburban units, 4001 and 4002, built in 1949. On 1.6.61 they formed a Charing Cross to Dartford service, one of the regular duties which they could perform, but the experiment was only partially successful and no further double-deck sets were authorized. The inset luggage doors next to the cab were just one of many unusual features.

Author

Generations of rail passengers travelling to and from the Continent have used Victoria as the London terminal. On 16.4.61 those who crossed from Calais to Folkestone during the morning arrived at platform 1 behind rebuilt 'Battle of Britain' 'Pacific' No. 34088 *213 Squadron*. The carriage immediately behind the tender was a Maunsell 'Nondescript' brake, regularly employed in boat trains.

Author

On the former 'Chatham' side of Victoria could be seen the boat train services linking London with the Continent, particularly France and Belgium. On 3.6.61 the Dover train was formed of new 4–CEP units, while original 'Spam Can' 'Battle of Britain' 4–6–2 No. 34067 *Tangmere* simmered in the sunshine alongside. After years in Barry scrapyard, *Tangmere* is being restored for active service once again on the Mid-Hants Steam Railway during the 1990s.

Author

Starting in the cavernous interior of the 'Brighton' side of Victoria, 'Standard' 4MT 2–6–4T No. 80014 burst into daylight with a train for Tunbridge Wells West via Oxted on 6.5.61. Most of this class of 155 engines was turned out by Brighton Works between 1951 and 1958, the first examples allocated to the Southern rapidly causing the withdrawal of any lingering LBSCR 4–4–2T and 4–6–2T designs (I3, J1, J2); some of these 'Standard' tanks remained at work until the very end of steam on the Southern in July 1967. Fortunately, several examples have been (or are being) restored for use on preserved lines around the country.

Author

The stock for the 'Golden Arrow' drifts down Grosvenor Bank into Victoria behind push-pull fitted 'Standard' 2MT 2–6–2T No. 84022 on 3.6.61, the sunshine highlighting the superb umber and cream Pullman carriages. A pair of green-painted Maunsell four-wheeled vans are provided for passengers' luggage instead of a corridor bogie van, and at this late stage the Pullman brake seems to have been dispensed with too.

Author

For the final days of its steam-hauled existence, the 'Golden Arrow' was in the capable care of rebuilt 'West Country' 4–6–2 No. 34100 *Appledore*. On 3.6.61 this superbly turned-out locomotive made a stirring assault on Grosvenor Bank at the head of a substantial load of Pullmans, strengthened by some additional Bulleid carriages and a new bogie GUV. Just eight days later, the same engine worked the last steam-hauled 'Arrow' to the Kent coast; thereafter, until the Pullmans finally ceased running, haulage was by electric or diesel power. It was the beginning of the end. . . .

Author

Past the 'searchlight' signal, Hawksworth 0–6–0PT No. 9410 plods steadily into platform 2 with empty carriage stock for another departure from Paddington on 17.5.61. Only the first ten examples of this class (9400–9409) were equipped with superheated boilers, the other 200 being non-superheated. No. 9400 is now preserved.

Author

In the bitter weather conditions that characterized the start of 1963, Hawksworth outside-cylinder pannier tank No. 1506 brought a train of 'Standard' Mark I stock into the terminus on 10 January. The 1500 class of heavy 0–6–0PT consisted of just ten engines, several of which were generally involved in ECS duties around the Western Region's only London terminal.

Author

The largest and, arguably, the most charismatic of the diesel-hydraulic locomotives put into service by the Western Region was the Western series introduced in 1961. When first built, most of the class appeared in Maroon livery but a handful were painted in the familiar Brunswick Green: No. D1035 *Western Yeoman* was one of these. When still quite new, No. D1035 stood throbbing at the head of a Birmingham express on 10.1.63 while evidence of the arctic conditions prevailing lingered on the platforms and between the rails.

Author

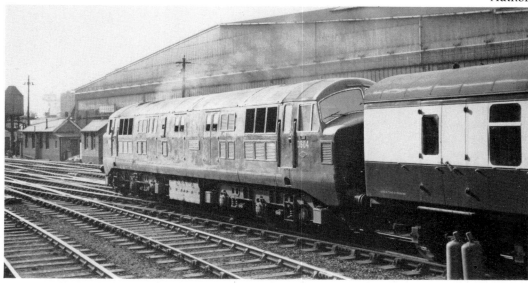

The earliest series of main line diesel-hydraulics was a group of five constructed in 1958 by the North British Locomotive Company with three-axle bogies (A1A–A1A). The D600–604 batch of 'Warship' locomotives was always non-standard and soon became exiled to Cornwall where Laira could keep a close watch on them. Before the arrival of the more powerful 'Westerns', No. D604 *Cossack* gives tongue with the 5.50 p.m. from Paddington to Plymouth ('The Mayflower') on 13.5.61; the Mark I carriages are in traditional GWR livery of Chocolate and Cream.

Author

The more familiar 'Warship' style, inspired by the DB V200 series, coasts gently in with an 'Up' West of England express on 3.6.61: D849 *Superb* was produced by the North British Locomotive Company not long before, and still gleams with fresh paint on what may well have been its first visit to the capital.

Author

Another Great Western tradition was soon to come to an end: on 28.10.58 as the 3.30 p.m. for Penzance gathered speed behind No. 6012 *King Edward VI*, one of the final slip carriage workings brought up the rear of the train. At Castle Cary the carriage was 'slipped' while the main train continued at speed; after being brought to a standstill in the station by the guard, the slip carriage was attached to an ordinary service train and arrived at Weymouth (Town) at 7 p.m. The very last slip working occurred on the Birmingham line in 1960.

Author

On 3.3.61 the 1.15 p.m. to Weston-super-Mare contained a most interesting restaurant car. Built in Churchward's time (1907) as one of a batch of twelve, W9540W was modernized in 1936 with new bogies and bigger windows. This 70 ft long carriage looked very quaint marshalled next to a 'Standard' Mark I coach, particularly as it retained the original roof pattern and some of the panelling. Part of Paddington's roof over platform 1 was under repair at the time.

Author

Ready for the 1.15 p.m. departure, 'Castle' class 4–6–0 No. 7017 *G J Churchward* was maintaining the very best of the Great Western traditions as it waited at platform 1 with train 1B11 for Weston-super-Mare one wintry day in March 1961. The long-established practice of smokebox reporting numbers was modified by the Western Region to allow for a route letter to be incorporated, though this meant omitting the first number of the standard four-digit code used by diesels and electrics (except on the Southern) – on express duty it was '1'.

Author

Three-in-one scene at Paddington on 2.6.61: 4–6–0 No. 6021 *King Richard II* headed train 1V03; 7MT 4–6–2 No. 70024 *Vulcan*, the 3.55 p.m. 'Capitals United Express'; and an unidentified 'Warship' diesel-hydraulic was at the front of the 4.05 p.m. for Plymouth. The 'Britannia' 'Pacific' was the first to leave.

Author

Steam's 'Indian summer': gleaming 4–6–0 No. 6027 *King Richard I* drifted in majestically on 15.4.61 in charge of the 'Up' 'Cambrian Coast Express', passing the first of the Swindon-built 'Warship' class diesel-hydraulics (D800 *Sir Brian Robertson*) beneath Bishop's Bridge Road. In less than two years the 'Kings' had left the stage. . . .

Author

On 13.3.61 platform 4 was host to the 'Birmingham Pullman' service, due to depart at 12.10 p.m. Passengers were required to pay a supplement of 10s. (50p) First Class and 5s. (25p) Second Class for the privilege of travelling on this train, each way. The eight-car diesel-electric unit was painted in a special livery of Nanking Blue and White; one of the power cars in this set was W60096.

Author

With red-liveried Underground stock of the Metropolitan Line nearby, 'Large Prairie' No. 6127 was preparing to remove empty stock from platform 9 on 15.4.61. Boys of all ages thronged wherever steam was in action around the station.

Author

The rasping exhaust of a double-chimney 'King': four-cylinder 4–6–0 No. 6022 *King Edward III* blasts away from platform 4 on 17.5.61 with the 6.10 p.m. to Birkenhead. Against the white smoke the double-chimney shows up clearly – this modification was carried out to all thirty of the 'Kings' and some of the 'Castles', as well as the thirty two-cylinder 'Counties' during the 1950s.

Author

A brace of 'Castles' at platforms 1 and 2 on 13.5.61. No. 4082 *Windsor Castle* storms past its class-mate (numbered in the 70xx series) with the 5.55 p.m. to Cardiff, Swansea and Carmarthen ('The Red Dragon'). Formerly No. 7013 *Bristol Castle*, this engine assumed the identity of No. 4082 *Windsor Castle* at the time of the death of King George VI in February 1952, as the real 4082 was in the Works having a major overhaul, so that it could work the King's funeral train.

Author

Empty stock for one of the important express services is brought into platform 4 on 15.4.61 by condensing pannier tank No. 9702. The Mark 1 carriages are painted in traditional Chocolate and Cream GWR colours, a concession granted for 'named' trains on the Western Region after abandonment of the previous Carmine and Cream colours in 1956.

Author

Turning the scales at around $58\frac{1}{4}$ tons, the 1500 class outside-cylinder pannier tanks were the heaviest of all the Western Region's large collection of 0–6–0PTs. Together with the other Hawksworth design (the 9400 type), these engines were given a 'Red' route restriction – the same as a 'Castle' or a 'Hall', for example – which limited their availability. No. 1507 was completely at home on Paddington ECS duties, being close to the buffer-stops at platform 4 on 13.3.61.

Author

The well-balanced design of the 2–6–2T is apparent from this broadside angle of 'Large Prairie' No. 6132, lifting empty stock out of the terminus on 17.5.61. After 1956, the approved livery for this type of engine was fully lined-out Brunswick Green.

Author

By the buffer-stops of platforms 1 and 2 could be seen examples of longitudinal sleepering of track, the sort of thing that was commonplace long ago. 2–6–2T No. 6132 was simmering quietly in platform 2 while activity was going on all around. In the background the Birkenhead service was loading up in platform 4. The date was 9.3.61.

Author

Next to the concourse, beside platform 4, 0–6–0PT No. 9702 was framed by the elegant arches of Paddington's classical architecture on 15.4.61 after it had brought in an ECS train. On the left, in platform 3, stood some elderly bogie vans while on the right, in platform 6, a modern diesel railcar unit throbbed with life. This was Paddington in the last days of steam. . . .

Author

There is a saying 'Last in, first out'; it was very nearly true of Marylebone. Youngest of the main line termini, for the Great Central did not reach London until the turn of the century, it became little more than a railhead for commuters from the Chiltern line once the Beeching Plan severed passenger trafffic north of Aylesbury. But all this was in the future when class N5 0–6–2T No. 69341 was engaged in carriage piloting on 15.2.58, with not a diesel railcar unit in sight.

Author

Gresley's masterpiece, the world-beating class A4 'Pacific' No. 60022 *Mallard* was displayed in immaculate condition at the exhibition on 14.5.61. Two years later it was withdrawn, restored to original condition with valances over the wheels and motion, and 'mothballed' for many years as part of the NRM collection. In this picture No. 60022 was in normal BR Brunswick Green livery.

Author

On 14.5.61 the Institution of Locomotive Engineers celebrated its Golden Jubilee in some style with an exhibition of various kinds of motive power, old and new, in sidings adjoining Marylebone station. Photography was not a simple matter until the crowds dispersed, but this view of the entrance shows 'Midland Compound' No. 1000 (with A4 *Mallard* behind) and on the left three-cylinder 'Pacific' No. 71000 *Duke of Gloucester*.

Author

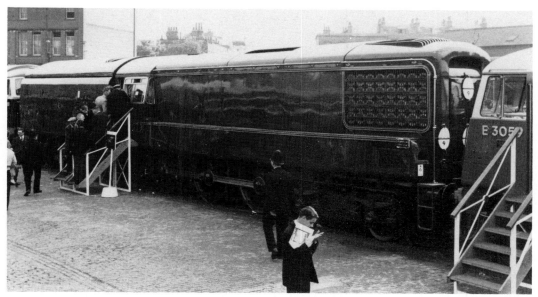

A most intriguing exhibit was the experimental Gas Turbine locomotive GT3, built and owned by the English Electric Company. Using a steam locomotive chassis (a 4–6–0 based on the 'Standard' 5MT designed at Doncaster), the finished product was painted in a pleasant shade of brown; it featured hinged headcode discs at the front as used on some pilot scheme BR diesels.

Author

A group of railway personnel pose in front of the preserved Midland Railway class 4P compound 4–4–0 No. 1000 (BR No. 41000) at the close of the exhibition on 14.5.61. Beautifully restored to MR condition, No. 1000 was painted in the handsome Crimson Lake that influenced the newly-formed LMS from 1923 onwards; it could also be said to have influenced the London Midland Region of BR from 1956 onwards, when twenty of the 8P 'Pacifics' were decked out in red paintwork for Anglo-Scottish expresses. It may also have been in the minds of those who decreed that the 'Western' and 'Warship' diesel-hydraulic locomotives of the Western Region should be painted maroon in the 1960s!

Author

Penultimate 'Pacific': 8P 4–6–2 No. 46256 *Sir William A Stanier FRS* eases the Perth and Blackpool express away from platform 13 at 1.20 p.m. on 16.5.61. Painted in red livery, this engine was an H.G. Ivatt development of the original Stanier 'Princess Coronation' class with roller bearings and other refinements.

Author

One of the ubiquitous Stanier 'Black 5' 4–6–0s, No. 44680, bustles out of 'old Euston' with a van train on 16.5.61, before the onset of electrification and rebuilding work changed it out of all recognition.

Author

A reminder of 'old Euston': on 2.9.55 'Jubilee' class 4–6–0 No. 45742 *Connaught* reversed its train of 'Blood and custard' carriages past the end of the platform towards Camden bank, having disgorged its passengers. In near-immaculate Brunswick Green livery, this particular 'Jubilee' was notable for having a double-chimney at the time – a feature of the preserved No. 45596 *Bahamas* today.

Author

Contrasts on 16.5.61, when the first Type 1 diesel-electric (D8000) was shunting a very elderly six-wheel van on the arrival side at Euston. The six-wheel van had Mansell wheels! Yet the prototype D8000, with its steam-era headcode discs, is now part of the National Collection at York, having retired from active service as 20 050.

Author

Silent and alone at the buffer-stop in platform 12 on 16.5.61 was the Southern Region's prototype main line diesel, 10201. Together with its two contemporaries (10202/3) it had been transferred to the LM Region to work alongside the original 'twins', 10000/1. By this stage its main activity was on empty stock workings in and out of Euston and on certain semi-fast duties. Carriages for the 'Red Rose' were loading at platform 13, in the background.

Author

As steam is released into the cylinders, class 5MT 4–6–0 No. 44773 begins to get excursion train 1Z40 under way from platform 12 on 16.5.61, bound for St Helens. Being an 8A (Edge Hill) engine, this is the return working to Merseyside after a trip to London.

Author

The imposing bulk of the Southern's third, and most powerful, diesel locomotive (10203) purrs into platform 12 with empty stock on 16.5.61. With 1–Co–Co–1 wheelbase and able to develop 2,000 bhp, this was the inspiration for the Peak class (D1 etc). Note the headcode discs set for an ECS working.

Author

The green-liveried *City of Lichfield* (8P 'Pacific' No. 46250) gets to grips with the 1.00 p.m. departure for Glasgow (Central) on 16.5.61. 'The Mid-Day Scot' ran non-stop from Euston as far as Crewe; even hardened railwaymen pause for a moment to witness the spectacle of one of Stanier's fine locomotives leaving for the north in time-honoured fashion.

Author

A topic of mutual interest seems to be occupying the staff in the foreground, while shapely 'Pacific' tank No. 69824 brings an element of the Great Central to the Great Northern terminal on 12.4.58. Class A5 4–6–2T No. 69824 is fresh from overhaul and may be running-in at King's Cross before returning to its home shed at Immingham (40B).

Author

'Stretched' streamliner: the one and only class W1 4–6–4 No. 60700 waits its turn to disappear into the tunnels and make for Top Shed (34A) for turning and servicing on 12.4.58. This unique engine was rebuilt in 1937 from Gresley's experimental high-pressure four-cylinder compound with his more usual three-cylinder arrangement, but was always eclipsed by A3 and A4 'Pacifics'.

Author

With some of the carriages still wreathed in steam, class A4 4–6–2 No. 60013 *Dominion of New Zealand* has emerged from the tunnels to coast into King's Cross with an 'Up' express on 12.4.58. At that date 'Deltics' and 'HSTs', let alone 'Inter-City 225s', were still but figments of designers' fertile imaginations.

Author

On 18.3.61 class A3 4–6–2 No. 60044 *Melton* came home to King's Cross with an 'Up' express formed of matching Maroon stock. This locomotive had acquired a double-chimney, but was otherwise little changed from its original Gresley outline.

Author

Not, perhaps, the most elegant design of steam tank engine, the class J50 0–6–0T was still a useful machine for shunting. No. 68983 shuffled into King's Cross past a group of Brush Type 2 diesels on 28.2.61.

Author

The massive lines of Robinson's class A5 4–6–2T could be appreciated at close quarters on 12.4.58. No. 69824, newly overhauled, was in charge of empty stock at King's Cross on that date, a task for which the 5 ft 7 in driving wheels were eminently suited.

Author

A study in light and shade: the classic lines of an original Gresley 'Pacific' are revealed against the industrial backcloth of the gasworks on 12.4.58. Class A3 4–6–2 No. 60067 *Ladas* sidles past the platform ends at King's Cross having completed its coaling and watering in readiness for the next main line duty.

Author

As the age of steam was drawing to a close on the East Coast main line, the days of the Thompson mixed-traffic 2–6–4T locomotives were numbered. Class L1 No. 67779 was reduced to carriage piloting in the capital on 28.2.61, never having achieved the dominance of suburban traffic established by Gresley's 0–6–2T designs since the 1920s.

Author

No longer in the best of condition, class N2 0–6–2T No. 69541 wheezes into King's Cross with empty stock on 17.4.59. The engine represents the condensing N2/2 variant common in the London area, as this type could work through the Metropolitan Line tunnels to Moorgate.

Author

Glimpsed from a passing train, the evening sunshine glinted on the half-polished paintwork of class N2 0–6–2T No. 69520 at King's Cross on 11.9.60. The squat boiler mountings and condensing pipes of the N2/2 version are clearly visible in this broadside view.

Author

The arrival of brand-new 'Deltic' Type 5 diesel-electric No. D9001 on 18.3.61 at the head of the 'Up' 'Flying Scotsman' service caused a ripple of interest among the many observers on the various platforms. As yet unnamed, in due course this engine was christened *St Paddy*; later still, it was to become 55 001. Such is the high regard in which the 'Deltics' are held, even more than a decade after their long reign ended on the East Coast expresses, that they still attract crowds of enthusiasts whenever the preserved examples make guest appearances.

Author

Before vanishing north of the Border, some of the Type 2 diesels constructed by Birmingham RC&W Company operated in the King's Cross area. On 14.4.59 new No. D5319 (with D5303 behind) was at the stabling point beyond the platform ends at King's Cross station while several steam locomotives went about their accustomed business nearby. Both diesels, which had Sulzer six-cylinder engines of 1,160 bhp, became part of class 26 in due course (26 019 and 26 003, respectively).

Author

The only steam locomotive permitted to operate over British Rail main lines after August 1968 was Alan Pegler's privately preserved Gresley class A3 'Pacific', *Flying Scotsman*, since it had a contract that allowed this. On 20.10.68 No. 4472 ran from Doncaster to London, entering King's Cross station to the acclaim of hundreds of enthusiasts. It was impossible to get near the famous locomotive, but this view through one of the arches shows the sole surviving non-streamlined Gresley 4–6–2 after arrival at platform 10, with a Craven DMU and a host of admirers alongside.

Author

Peppercorn 'Pacific' No. 60130 *Kestrel* makes a dramatic exit on 18.3.61 with the 3.50 p.m. to Peterborough, the class Al's wheels spinning wildly for a moment on the greasy rails before coming under control enabling the big engine to make a more dignified departure. In the adjoining platform 'Britannia' class 7MT 4–6–2 No. 70041 *Sir John Moore* has charge of the 4.10 p.m. to Cleethorpes.

Author

Moment of departure: No. 70041 *Sir John Moore* steals forward with the 4.10 p.m. Cleethorpes express beneath the shadow of the great train shed. The Immingham-based 'Britannia' draws the attention of people of all ages, for there is a timeless appeal about steam that transcends any generation.

Author

Green locomotive, maroon carriage: with driving wheels spinning in an effort to get the heavy train moving towards the tunnels as quickly as possible, yet controlled to avoid damage, *Sir John Moore* has a clear road ahead with the 4.10 p.m. to Cleethorpes on 18.3.61. With tender piled high and the big engine in good condition, the lucky passengers have every prospect of an exciting run.

Author

Fourth-rail electric services operated across the top of London, linking Richmond, Willesden, Watford, Croxley Green, Euston and Broad Street. The last mentioned station had been the terminal for the North London Railway (absorbed into the LNWR in 1908), and LNWR Siemens and Oerlikon stock began working during the First World War. The last examples of North Western Oerlikon trains could be seen in the fifties at Broad Street; the station has now closed.

Lens of Sutton

There were two steam locomotives that regularly shunted around Liverpool Street whose paintwork and pipework warranted superlatives. On 30.4.58 class N7 0–6–2T No. 69614 was the engine involved, a former GER loco rebuilt in LNER days with round-top firebox.

Author

The other station pilot was a little class J69 'Buckjumper'. On 28.11.60 the blue-liveried 0–6–0T stood quietly simmering beneath the overhead wires, the GER coat of arms carried on the bunker sides below the number (68619); the BR emblem appeared as usual on the tank sides. Despite electrification of the suburban services, this terminal was very dark and cheerless, so the spotless steam engine could hardly have been a greater contrast!

Author

One of the inside-cylinder 4–6–0s of Great Eastern origin, class B12 No. 61549, was waiting by the platform signal on 16.3.55. The short tender contrasted with the length of the boiler barrel when viewed broadside on; the round-top boiler was a Gresley modification introduced in the 1930s on most of the class.

Author

Two of the B17 class 4–6–0s, side by side at Liverpool Street on 16.3.55. While 61645 *The Suffolk Regiment* had been modified with the B1 type boiler, classmate 61670 *City of London* had rather more drastic surgery: built in 1937 with streamlined casing (like a smaller version of Gresley's famous A4 design) for working the 'East Anglian' express, it had the streamlining removed and a new 100A boiler fitted in 1951.

Author

The evening sunlight illuminated one of the 'Footballers' on 2.5.59 as it stood beside the cab road in the middle of Liverpool Street. Class B17 4–6–0 No. 61666 *Nottingham Forest* was in Brunswick Green livery with 6 ft 8 in driving wheels and 4,200-gallon tender.

Author

All change at Liverpool Street: Type 4 diesel-electric D204 'whistles' past Type 2 D5515 on 30.9.58, while several steam locomotives make ready beside the cab road. The larger (1–Co–Co–1) diesel became 40 004 many years later, while the Brush design was renumbered 31 015. Note the water crane on the left.

Author

Once dieselization of East Anglian services began, steam's influence started to wane. On 30.9.58 the BR-built class K1 2–6–0 No. 62066 and 'Standard' 7MT 4–6–2 No. 70030 *William Wordsworth* still had jobs to do, but from this time on it was downhill all the way. . . .

Author

The legendary powers of acceleration of the GE suburban designs could be disconcerting at times. On 14.9.57 class N7 0–6–2T No. 69671 emerged slowly from the gloom within then, as the signal changed, it shot forward like a rocket! Beyond the wall of Liverpool Street was Broad Street station.

Author

Not active within the British Railways period, but displayed as part of the LT collection to mark the centenary of the opening of the Metropolitan Railway in 1863, Beyer Peacock 4–4–0T No. 23 appeared at Neasden depot on 26.5.63. Built in 1866 as a condensing tank – and one of the Metropolitan Railway's first locomotives – it was later fitted with a cab roof and ran on the Brill branch from Quainton Road until 1935 (when that line closed). It survived in traffic long enough to have the inscription LONDON TRANSPORT on the side tanks for its final period in service. The type was known as class A.

Author

Now also preserved is former Metropolitan Railway No. 1, built at Neasden in 1896. In London Transport days, after 1933, it was renumbered L.44 and continued to be active on departmental duties until the early 1960s. Maintained at the Buckinghamshire Railway Centre at Quainton Road, the 0–4–4T has been restored to Metropolitan Railway livery and has made occasional forays on to the London Underground network on special duties in recent years. This type was known as class E.

Author

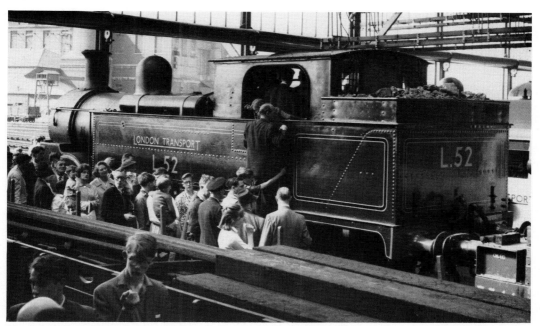

The Neasden exhibition in 1963 was the last opportunity for the public to admire the London Transport class F 0–6–2T No. L.52, for it was scrapped soon afterwards. Thereafter LT standardized on former Western Region 0–6–0PTs made redundant by BR, a policy that enabled steam to continue in use on the Metropolitan and District sections on departmental trains until 1971.

Author

Unless one was fortunate enough to have 'inside knowledge', it would have been quite by chance to see one of the London Transport steam-hauled goods trains. Such an opportunity occurred at Stamford Brook (LT) station in November 1969, when one of the red-liveried ex-WR panniers appeared on an Acton Works to Lillie Bridge duty. In the heat of the moment it was not possible to ascertain which engine it was!

Author

London Transport continued to employ elderly compartment stock on Metropolitan Line services between Aldgate and Watford as well as out to Aylesbury. The Watford T stock shown here (displayed at the Neasden Centenary Exhibition in 1963) was an electric-powered unit, whereas an electric (ex-Metropolitan) locomotive gave way to steam at Rickmansworth with the other stock. The Chesham branch was also steam operated, employing vintage Metropolitan push-pull coaches coupled to a BR locomotive until it, too, was electrified in 1961.

Author

From 1936 a connecting bus service was provided by London Transport between certain main line termini, using a special series of Leyland 'Cub' vehicle with 'observation' type bodywork. Painted blue and cream, these petrol-engined buses stood out from the normal red buses or Green Line coaches. 'Inter-Station' Cub C112 (CLX 549) waits hopefully for custom on 22.4.50, near the end of its working life.

Alan B. Cross

Surrounded by onlookers, London Transport 0–6–0PT No. L.94 brought the very last steam-hauled goods train to Neasden LT depot on 6.6.71 – on an overcast day, the engine puffed steadily through the station past one of the aluminium Underground trains. L.94 was purchased for preservation and has reverted to its original Great Western identity (7752) owned by Birmingham Railway Museum; it was built in 1930.

Author

The Suburbs and Beyond

SOUTH-WEST

As a twelve-coach express from Portsmouth Harbour nears Vauxhall, 0–6–0PT No. 4698 plods out of Waterloo with empty stock for Clapham Junction on 12.1.61. The train from Portsmouth consisted of three 4–COR 'Nelson' sets, travelling at almost 60 m.p.h. – not the smoothest of positions from which to photograph a moving 'target'.

Author

Stepping out smartly in spite of its age, Adams' 'Radial' (0415 class) No. 30582 passed through Queen's Road, Battersea station on 19.3.61 bound for Chertsey. The Decca building adjoining Stewarts Lane depot can be seen on the right. Queen's Road, Battersea has since been renamed Queenstown Road.

Author

With the sun low in the sky, 'King Arthur' 4–6–0 No. 30788 *Sir Urre of the Mount* was shunting vans and empty coaching stock at Clapham Junction on 14.4.59. Notice the old-style station name board on the left.

Author

A five-coach set of rather vintage non-corridor carriages leaves Clapham Junction for Kensington (Olympia) on 14.4.59. Set 636 appears to consist of ex-SECR stock while the motive power is provided by ex-LSWR Drummond M7 0–4–4T No. 30319. The entourage is passing beneath Clapham Junction 'A' box heading for Latchmere junction.

Author

One of the Southern's fastest trains, 'The Royal Wessex' screams through Clapham Junction behind rebuilt 'Merchant Navy' 4–6–2 No. 35025 *Brocklebank Line* on 14.4.59. Clapham Junction 'A' signal-box is on the gantry on the left while 'B' box is the brick structure on the right. The 4.35 p.m. from Waterloo regularly loaded to thirteen bogies, stopping only at Winchester City on the way to Southampton Central.

Author

On 5.6.66 'The Surrey Rambler' special train arrived at Kensington (Olympia) with rebuilt 'Merchant Navy' *Clan Line*. After reversal, the excursion set off behind 'Standard' 4MT 2–6–4T No. 80154. This was the last steam locomotive to have been constructed at Brighton Works – while many of its contemporaries have been saved from scrap, regrettably this was not one of them. The fourth-rail London Transport track is on the left of the picture.

Author

On 14.8.66 an 'Up' van train passed Woking with 'Standard' 4MT 2–6–0 No. 76031 in charge. This engine had spent the early period of its existence on the Midland and Great Northern section, having the cab-sides cut away for single-line tablet apparatus to be fitted.

Author

A remarkable farewell tour was organized for two of the three surviving Beattie well-tanks on 2.12.62, from Waterloo to Hampton Court. After pausing at Surbiton, the two veterans of 1874, Nos. 30585/7, made a dignified departure from platform 1. The tour was so popular it had to be repeated a fortnight later, when the pair of 2–4–0WTs coupled bunker to bunker.

Author

In abysmal external condition, rebuilt 'Battle of Britain' 4–6–2 No. 34077 *603 Squadron* powered through Basingstoke at speed on 27.8.66 with the 'Down' 'Bournemouth Belle', its whistle wailing in typical Bulleid fashion. The third rail was already in position for the forthcoming electrification, but it was not energized until some months later. The 'Standard' 'BG' full brake behind the tender had been painted in Pullman livery to match the carriages, as no Pullman brake was available.

Author

With the end of steam on the Southern only five weeks away, 'Standard' class 5MT 4–6–0 No. 73092 roared through Brookwood on 3.6.67 with an 'Up' express. While the external appearance of the engine was nothing short of deplorable, its mechanical condition gave no cause for concern. The four-track section between Worting junction and Woking was the South-Western Division's acknowledged 'race track' where speeds into three figures were known to have been achieved from time to time! Brookwood was formerly the junction for the Bisley branch, away to the right of this picture; on the opposite side of the line was the Necropolis cemetery, which also had its own private sidings and station in days gone by.

Author

The first of two special trains to be sponsored by Ian Allan (the well-known transport publishers) ran to Ashford Works on 5.4.61 behind a pair of vintage 4–4–0s. Class T9 No. 30117 piloted E1 No. 31019 through Waterloo (East) on this date, the 'Greyhound' having been brought out of store at Eastleigh specially for the purpose.

Author

At Grove Park station on 3.11.57 engineers were carrying out routine Sunday maintenance to the track. Class C 0–6–0 No. 31717 had been earmarked for the engineers train, so the old engine was in light steam ready to move when needed. Only very rarely in those days were substitute bus services required, because British Railways continued to run trains (to a modified timetable, if necessary) *around* the track work.

Author

The second Ian Allan excursion to Ashford Works ran on 12.4.61. The pairing of 4–4–0s was subtly changed, with the 1899-built 'Greyhound' T9 leading class D1 No. 31749 on this occasion. Both former express engines had a good head of steam as they ran gently through platform C at Waterloo (East), having set out from Charing Cross under yellow signals. At one stage 30117 was the preferred option as an example of the famous Drummond design to be kept for the National Collection, but in the end the choice fell upon 30120 (LSWR No. 120) which is now on loan to the Purbeck Line at Swanage.

Author

In London and the suburbs, the trams were an institution with some routes running all night. On 14.10.50 one of the bogie cars (believed to be 1308) was working the 36 route at New Cross Gate station, providing a useful connection with the Victoria Embankment, Elephant & Castle or Greenwich. The trams ceased operating on 5.7.52 – who knows, perhaps a modernized system might be set up in time for the New Millenium?

Alan B. Cross

In recent times the smart new image of Network South-East has brought many changes in its wake. But even before that, stations were being altered and old landmarks obliterated. The signal-box at Merstham, on the old Brighton Line north of Redhill, was recorded shortly before demolition, having been made redundant through the installation of area panel boxes. The Quarry Line, avoiding Redhill, is in the background.

Author

Spring was in the air on 3.3.57 as Maunsell's last style of inside-cylinder 4–4–0, the L1 class, made an unexpected foray along the Swanley junction – Maidstone East – Ashford line. No. 31753 was the lowest numbered member of the class, built in 1926; it was spotted approaching Offham Crossing just before midday.

Author

By 1961 the writing was on the wall for the delightful branch line from Dunton Green to Westerham. On 21 October class H 0–4–4T No. 31263 was providing the motive power for the push-pull service, pausing at Brasted Halt with the 12.50 p.m. for Westerham only days before closure. The Wainwright tank engine was saved and continues to be active on the Bluebell Railway not far away from its old haunts.

Author

Sometimes on Sundays, if the main line through Tonbridge was closed for engineering works, the Swanley junction – Maidstone East – Ashford line might be used for diversions. On 28.7.57 several passenger services came that way, but one of the most interesting sights was a horse-box special headed towards London: class L1 4–4–0 No. 31755 passed Offham Crossing with a clean exhaust in spite of the adverse gradient.

Author

While steam on the standard gauge was approaching its end in June 1967, there did not appear to be any immediate threat to the narrow gauge (2 ft 6 in/76 cm gauge) system between Sittingbourne and Ridham Dock on the banks of the River Swale. Serving the Bowater Paper Mills, it had a number of small steam engines still at work, like this Bagnall 0–6–2T *Triumph*, complete with spark arrester chimney and headlamp. Such a locomotive would not look out of place on the NG lines of Europe (particularly in Austria), but it has been preserved on part of the original system at Sittingbourne. Note the timber trucks.

Author

Completely different in appearance was Kerr Stuart 0–6–2T *Superior* whose green paintwork and neat lining-out was a joy to behold in 1967 when steam on BR was breathing its last. Notice the oil cans and cotton waste conveniently to hand – no wonder this engine was so clean! It is preserved today at Whipsnade on the 2 ft 6 in gauge system established there.

Author

The most unusual of the Sittingbourne narrow-gauge engines was, appropriately, *Unique*. A 2–4–0T (or is it an 0–4–2T?) built by Bagnall for the 2 ft 6 in gauge system, *Unique* was a fireless loco. In June 1967 it was in steam and, shortly after this photograph was taken, moved off to another part of the paper mill. It, too, has been preserved on its native system in north Kent.

Author

A curious little 0–4–0ST that once worked as the Retort locomotive at Beckton gasworks has been saved, in the shape of Neilson's No. 5087 (Beckton No. 25). For a time it was stored at the Bluebell Railway in East Sussex – where it was photographed – but it has since found a permanent home at Bressingham Gardens in East Anglia.

Author

Two of the 'Quad-Art' sets made up the Fenchurch Street to Tilbury service hauled by three-cylinder Stanier 4MT 2–6–4T No. 42521 on 14.10.58. Work was in hand to prepare the line for overhead electrification, but this did not seem to impede passenger traffic at Barking.

Author

As the shadows lengthen, 'Britannia' class 7MT 'Pacific' No. 70040 *Clive of India* clatters over the points at Bethnal Green on 2.5.59 with an 'Up' express for Liverpool Street. Steam 'under the wires' did not seem to cause any problems here!

Author

Freight operation on the Tilbury line was beginning to see diesel power: on 14.10.58 Brush Type 2 No. D5506 studiously avoided the fourth-rail London Transport tracks as it drifted through Barking with a very mixed goods. The headcode discs made an interesting feature.

Author

The three-cylinder 4MT 2–6–4Ts used on many of the Tilbury services to or from Fenchurch Street could show a fair turn of speed, especially when they did not stop at the intermediate stations served by London Transport. On 2.5.59 No. 42534 surged past West Ham bound for Fenchurch Street with an afternoon service made up of non-corridor stock, including some modern BR-built examples.

Author

Darkening the sky with a rush-hour Tilbury service from Fenchurch Street on 2.5.59, Stanier three-cylinder 2–6–4T No. 42518 charges the adverse gradient past West Ham station with the usual eight non-corridor coaches. The industrial landscape of this part of east London had an appeal all its own, but recent development along the lower reaches of the Thames has changed it greatly.

Author

Based upon a sound, simple design by Worsdell for the GER in 1883, the class J15 0–6–0s inherited by British Railways were still very useful engines, especially on the light traffic routes of rural East Anglia. The late-Victorian ancestry of No. 65476 gave it a certain charm, especially when it had been well burnished for the special excursion around the suburban lines on 7.4.62. With a modern EMU in the adjoining platform, the old engine had a good head of steam when it made ready to leave Chingford for the next stage of the tour.

Author

On the morning of 28.2.59 Stanier 8F 2–8–0 No. 48370 shuffled past Neasden junction with a partly-fitted freight for Cricklewood. On the right is Neasden shed (34E) while in the background, beyond the junction signals, can be seen the cooling towers of the power station at Willesden. In addition to goods traffic, this route carried excursion trains bound for the Midland main line.

Author

After the formation of London Transport in 1933 there was a gradual expansion of electrification using Underground rolling stock. The Ongar branch was one that had to wait until after the formation of British Railways before steam gave way to the Tube. At Epping station in the early 1950s contrasts like this might be seen, with class F5 2–4–2T No. 67202 towering over a Central Line train for Loughton. The F5 was push-pull fitted to avoid having to run-round its train; part of the apparatus was attached to the side of the smokebox.

Lens of Sutton

Occasionally, a non push-pull locomotive was given the Epping to Ongar duty. Seen running-round at Ongar in the early fifties, class F5 2–4–2T No. 67212 was a condensing example of Holden's design; the large end windows of the driving compartment of the push-pull set show up clearly in the bright sunshine.

Lens of Sutton

The terminus at Ongar as it was in steam days: a simple platform with the usual facilities, gas lighting, a characteristic signal-box to control the few crossover points and sidings plus a small engine shed. The branch engine, with bunker full of coal, can just be discerned inside.

Lens of Sutton

Another branch line in the London area that did not have such a happy outcome was from South Tottenham to Seven Sisters and Palace Gates, closing from 7.1.63. A push-pull service was at the terminus of Palace Gates in this view, the set being numbered 132–A.

Lens of Sutton

The former Great Northern branch to Alexandra Palace had a chequered career: it was closed and re-opened twice before finally ceasing operation in July 1954. Class N2 0–6–2T No. 69535 was in charge of the branch train when this picture was taken at Alexandra Palace, but the station appeared almost deserted.

Lens of Sutton

Looking rather travel-stained, class A4 'Pacific' No. 60008 *Dwight D. Eisenhower* ambles through Finsbury Park in the direction of King's Cross on 28.2.61. In the background several new Brush diesels can be seen, indicating that the era of steam on the East Coast main line is drawing to a close.

Author

A push-pull train leaves Alexandra Palace station behind as it is propelled past the fine GN junction signal in the direction of Finsbury Park. Apart from the elaborate building, the rest of the scene looks surprisingly rural – forty years ago!

Lens of Sutton

With a relatively easy load of nine bogies, class A1 4–6–2 No. 60153 *Flamboyant* coasts through Finsbury Park with a Saltburn to King's Cross service on 28.2.61. 60153 was a roller-bearing engine, still remarkably clean for the period.

Author

In dull weather class A3 4–6–2 No. 60049 *Galtee More* hustles the 'Northumbrian' express through Finsbury Park on the final stage of its long journey on 28.2.61. The older style of tender contrasts oddly with the double-chimney and German type of smoke deflectors fitted not long before to this venerable 'Pacific'.

Author

During a brief stop at Bishop's Stortford while aboard a Liverpool Street to Cambridge service on 16.3.55 this class J17 0–6–0 was seen shunting in the goods yard. Bishop's Stortford used to be the junction for Dunmow and Braintree until three years before, when the passenger service was withdrawn. No. 65535 still found employment on pick up goods duties for several more years.

Author

Once a familiar sight on many semi-fast and secondary passenger trains in East Anglia, the 'Claud Hamilton' type of 4–4–0 as improved in the thirties had a very pleasing line to it. Classified D16 in LNER days, there were a number of variations within the class: No. 62571 of Cambridge (31A) featured the modified footplating over the massive 7 ft 0 in diameter driving wheels when recorded on 16.3.55.

Author

133

On the four-track Great Northern main line heading for New Southgate on 18.6.62 was a somewhat uneconomic freight operation, comprising class 8F 2–8–0 No. 90000 with a solitary cattle van and the brake. The locomotive was one of the 'WD' series built for war service in 1943 – after seeing a brief period on loan to the Dutch railways in 1946, WD No. 77009 was sold to the LNER and became No. 3000 in December of that year. Much of its time in BR days was spent at Colwick, but by this date it was based at Hornsey (34B); 90000 was withdrawn from Frodingham depot in 1965 and scrapped.

Author

With an insistent rhythm from the short-wheelbase wagons passing over the rail joints, class 5MT 4–6–0 No. 45285 thunders through Elstree and Borehamwood on 18.3.61. The fast tracks are on the right, with new trackwork stored temporarily in between the two sets of Midland main lines.

Author

Diesel parcels cars were introduced by the Great Western in the 1930s, but with the BR Modernization Plan the LM Region decided to follow suit. On 18.3.61 one of the new cars (M55989) was approaching Elstree and Borehamwood on its way north from London; constructed by the Gloucester RC&W Company with BUT (Leyland/Albion) engines, it had mechanical transmission and weighed 40 tons.

Author

A very assorted parcels train motored through the 'Up' slow platform of Elstree and Borehamwood station on 18.3.61 with BR-built Type 2 loco No. D5086 in charge. In later years it was renumbered 24 086, after the livery changed from Brunswick Green to all-over blue (with yellow ends).

Author

One of the handsome and highly successful class 9F 2–10–0 locomotives, No. 92086, wheels an unfitted goods through Elstree and Borehamwood on 18.3.61, the driver taking the opportunity to open the regulator as soon as the engine is clear of the station footbridge. This 9F has a 15B (Kettering) shedplate.

Author

As the new 'Peak' diesels were infiltrating the Midland main line, it was something of a lottery which engine might work the train. But on 18.3.61 a St Pancras – Nottingham express managed to produce 'Royal Scot' class 7P 4–6–0 No. 46112 *Sherwood Forester*, a highly suitable choice, as it left the tunnels behind to roar through Elstree and Borehamwood station.

Author

Doyen of the class, 7P 4–6–0 No. 46100 *Royal Scot* hurtled past Elstree and Borehamwood with an 'Up' Bradford express for St Pancras on the afternoon of 18.3.61. The station architecture helped to epitomize the steam age on the Midland main line, an era that was so soon to pass into history. By good fortune this fine locomotive can be seen today at Bressingham Gardens near Diss, where it has been restored in the pre-war Crimson Lake livery of the LMS.

Author

Many of the Fowler class 3 2–6–2Ts spent the bulk of their working lives in the London area, some being equipped with condensing apparatus for working through the tunnels to Moorgate. No. 40020, on the other hand, was fitted with push-pull control gear when at Bedford (15D) on 25.4.59, something more often associated with the Ivatt class 2 (412xx) series.

Author

A representative of the old order could be found lurking among the goods sidings at Bedford on 25.4.59. With smokebox daubed with black bitumen and the chimney covered over with sacking to keep out the damp, a rebuilt Midland Railway veteran from the Victorian years served as a reminder of how things used to be. Class 2F 0–6–0 No. 58214 had the larger (5 ft 3 in diameter) driving wheels, a Belpaire firebox and improved cab, and was surrounded with old private-owner coal wagons more than ten years after Nationalization.

Author

The former MR branch between Bedford and Hitchin was one of the nearest places to London that it was possible to find a four-wheel Railbus at work. Built by Park Royal and powered by a 150 bhp AEC engine, M79972 seated fifty passengers and weighed 15 tons. The experiment was rather short-lived, for the branch was closed from 1.1.62, but at Bedford (Midland Road) station on 25.4.59 it was a novel experience.

Author

For a time the Midland main line was the stamping ground of the new Metro-Vick Type 2 'Co-Bo' diesel-electrics. Only twenty were built and their exposure on top-link duties was brief. On 25.4.59 an 'Up' express for St Pancras was double-headed by D5707 and D5712, seen passing the locomotive depot at speed. The repeating Home and Distant arms of the semaphore signals on the right are worthy of note.

Author

It used to be rather a tradition of the Midland in days gone by to double-head the more important trains. This practice had grown up because the Midland had a 'small engine' policy pre-1923 and the habit stuck. . . . On 25.4.59 a St Pancras – Bradford express rocketed past Bedford MPD with a superannuated 2P 4–4–0 (No. 40504) piloting 'Jubilee' class 4–6–0 No. 45622 *Nyasaland*. The class 2P was not one of the 1928 series built under Fowler's direction but a Johnson rebuild having high-stepping driving wheels of 7 ft 0½ in diameter; the 'Jubilee' had to make do with 6 ft 9 in drivers.

Author

As 1962 slipped away, the grip of modern mainline diesels on many of the most important duties became more and more apparent. On 22.12.62 the 'Red Rose' express from Euston had Type 4 English Electric D309 up front, its steam-heating boiler working overtime as the train passed through Watford Junction. In later years this 'Whistler' was renumbered 40 109.

Author

In the winter sunshine of 22.12.62 duty 1K25 was entrusted to steam haulage. Rebuilt 'Patriot' class 7P 4–6–0 No. 45529 *Stephenson* was in good fettle for the semi-fast from Euston to Crewe as it ran into the platform at Watford Junction, the train consisting of some very comfortable corridor stock of LMS parentage. Having taken this picture, the author dashed across to the appropriate platform and was able to enjoy a lively journey behind *Stephenson* as far as Bletchley – a fitting finale for steam on the erstwhile LNWR main line.

Author

On a misty autumn morning a special railtour was run from Marylebone to Nottingham, which brought to the London area a type of locomotive more usually associated with the north-east of England. Class B16 4–6–0 No. 61438 was a Gresley rebuild (B16/2 variant) of the Raven mixed-traffic design for the NER, substituting Walschaerts valve gear for the original Stephenson pattern. On 14.10.62 the three-cylinder beat made stirring music as 61438 worked hard through Aylesbury, encouraged by a good head of steam.

Author

Aylesbury station with two Chiltern Line four-car DMU sets in the platforms and a third unit in the former steam locomotive depot on the left; Aylesbury was a sub-shed of 34E (Neasden). Since 5.9.66 this former Metropolitan and Great Central Joint station has been the northern terminus of passenger services from Marylebone, following closure of the through route via Calvert, Woodford and Rugby Central.

Author

A pair of WR push-pull carriages was being propelled into Princes Risborough past the North signal-box on 3.4.60. Princes Risborough was formerly the junction for Watlington and Oxford, as well as for Aylesbury (which remains open), on the main line to Banbury.

Author

One of the familiar 'Large Prairie' 2–6–2T engines, No. 6111, was in charge of an Oxford to Princes Risborough local train on 3.4.60. The single line route served a number of rural stations and halts along the Thames Valley until closure from 7.1.63.

Author

The Watlington branch lost its passenger services from 1.7.57, but the line remained open for freight. This was the country terminus station on 3.4.60, when a special train of two auto-coaches was propelled by 0–4–2T No. 1473. The GWR carriage nearer the camera was W172W, a Diagram A.28 auto-trailer of 1930.

Author

This period picture of the Watlington branch shows 0–4–2T No. 1473 (in lined Brunswick Green livery) bustling through the remote Aston Rowant station on 3.4.60 with two auto-trailers in tow, bound for Princes Risborough. Even though passenger traffic ceased almost three years before, the 9 mile branch retained a freight service throughout at this stage, with intermediate stations and halts virtually unchanged; in later years it was cut back to Chinnor only, for the Rugby cement traffic, but has since closed completely.

Author

Hauling what was believed to be its first special passenger train – 'The Six Counties Limited' – 9F 2–10–0 No. 92220 pounded through Bledlow on the Princes Risborough – Oxford line with duty 1X07 on 3.4.60. *Evening Star* was the last steam locomotive to be constructed for British Railways, being built at Swindon in March 1960. The country station and simple goods yard (with crane and timber loading gauge) represent a bygone age.

Author

The short winter's day was drawing in as class 5100 2–6–2T No. 4103 raised the echoes leaving Horspath Halt with an afternoon train from Princes Risborough to Oxford on 12.12.59. The steam heating was working inside and outside the carriages!

Author

Shuffling past Westbourne Park station on 10.1.63, Hawksworth outside-cylinder pannier tank 1506 was removing some empty stock from Paddington during the exceptionally cold spell. The distinctive 'searchlight' type of colour light signals can be seen by the platform ramp.

Author

There was a steady procession of ECS trains in either direction passing Westbourne Park station throughout the day. On 17.5.61 outside-cylinder 0–6–0PT No. 1505 plodded past during the afternoon as a Pressed Steel DMU with 'speed whiskers' headed towards Paddington.

Author

There were not many instances of double-heading in or out of Paddington in steam days, but the 2.55 p.m. to Swansea and Bristol was one such service. On 17.5.61 the combination involved 'Warship' diesel-hydraulic D832 *Onslaught* leading 'Castle' class 4–6–0 No. 7001 *Sir James Milne* past Westbourne Park; the 'Warship' had just been built at Swindon Works, being the last of the first series (D800–D832). A further batch of five (D866–D870) appeared from Swindon after the North British series (D833–D865) had entered stock. *Onslaught* is now preserved.

Author

The Twyford–Henley-on-Thames branch still maintained a proper GWR image in 1967. A single diesel-railcar, W55020 built by Pressed Steel with two AEC engines in 1960, paused at Wargrave to offload a handful of passengers on 30 November. Nicknamed 'Bubble-car', the Pressed Steel single unit is known as class 121.

Author

The Western Region had very few Departmental locomotives, all of them internal combustion machines. No. 20 was a small Ruston and Hornsby 0–4–0D diesel-mechanical weighing just 17 tons; the four-cylinder engine developed only 88 bhp and the transmission was chain driven. It was based from 1957 until closure at Reading Signal Depot.

Author

Going out in style: on 5.2.67 the 'South Western Suburban Rail Tour' visited Reading General and the Coley branch (Central Goods), being the 100th railtour organized by the Locomotive Club of Great Britain. Standard 4MT 2–6–0 No. 76058 powered the excursion, and provided a dramatic (and noisy) exit beneath the girder bridge carrying the A4 trunk road as it set out to return to Reading General.

Author

Survivors and Specialities

For a few years Londoners and others willing to travel to Clapham could enjoy a wide variety of historic transport on display in the former London Transport tram depot. The display included tramcars, buses, trolleybuses and railway artefacts – many of which had been stored away out of sight for years. One of those to see the light of day was the LNWR 2–4–0 No. 790 *Hardwicke*, one of Webb's 'Precedent' class built in 1892. In the left background can be seen the little LBSCR 'Terrier' 0–6–0T, *Boxhill*.

Author

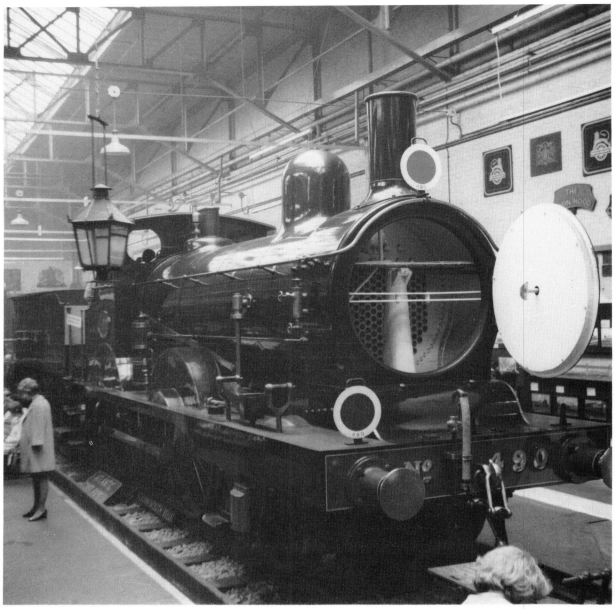

Another inhabitant of Clapham was Britain's last operational 2–4–0 tender locomotive – GER No. 490 (BR No. 62785). Designated by the LNER as class E4, this engine was built in 1894 and remained active until 1958 on branch lines in East Anglia. The open smokebox offers a rare view of the boiler tubes – note the 'stovepipe' chimney.

Author

An appropriate exhibit at Clapham was the erstwhile SECR class D 4–4–0 No. 737, built in 1901. With all its copper and brasswork as well as a most intricate livery, this engine was always of great interest. When new it headed boat trains for the Channel ports; in old age it pulled local passenger services between Reading, Guildford and Redhill, being retired from Guildford (70C) numbered 31737 in 1956. In the foreground a miniature steam loco modelled on the NG former Corris Railway 0–4–2T *Edward Thomas* was trundling up and down on a short length of track to the delight of the children. Clapham closed in 1972 and the display was dispersed – most of the non-London railway exhibits to an enlarged National Railway Museum at York, the London items in due course to Covent Garden.

Author

This was the engine, this the train that broke the infamous 'Steam Ban'. On 7.10.71 a special steam-hauled train left Paddington station for Swindon Works: consisting of several Pullman cars provided by the Bulmers Cider Centre at Hereford, it was worked throughout by the celebrated 'flagship' of the Great Western, No. 6000 *King George V*, thus ending a famine of steam power on the main line since *Flying Scotsman* went to America. *KGV* was recorded near Pangbourne in the Thame Valley, heading west with the Pullmans making a brave show in the autumn sunshine; speed was estimated to be 50-plus, and rising. . . .

Author